Celebrate the incredible journey of Phoebe Waller-Bridge's outrageously funny, blazingly original *Fleabag*, from the fringe theatre hit to international cultural phenomenon, in this special edition—featuring the original playscript, never-before-seen color photos, exclusive content by Phoebe, director Vicky Jones, and key members of the creative team.

In 2013, *Fleabag* made its debut as a one-woman show in the sixty-seat Big Belly at the Edinburgh Festival Fringe's Underbelly. It was an immediate hit, going on to enjoy two runs at London's Soho Theatre, national and international tours, while picking up numerous prizes, including London's Critics' Circle Theatre Award, The Stage Edinburgh Award, a Fringe First Award, two West End Theatre Awards, and an Olivier Award nomination.

The 2016 TV adaptation propelled *Fleabag* and Phoebe to worldwide fame, earning critical acclaim and further accolades including Writers' Guild, Royal Television Society, and BAFTA Television Awards. A second series, nominated for eleven Emmy Awards, and winning six, including Outstanding Comedy Series, Lead Actress, and Writing followed in 2019, along with a sold-out run of the original play in New York.

This special edition is released alongside *Fleabag*'s first West End run at Wyndham's Theatre, London. It is introduced by Deborah Frances-White, stand-up comedian, writer, and host of *The Guilty Feminist* podcast.

FLEABAG

FLEABAG

The Special Edition

Phoebe Waller-Bridge

THEATRE COMMUNICATIONS GROUP
NEW YORK
2019

Fleabag: The Special Edition is published by Theatre Communications Group, Inc., 520 Eighth Avenue, 24th Floor, New York, NY 10018-4156

This volume is published in arrangement with Nick Hern Books Limited, The Glasshouse, 49a Goldhawk Road, London W12 8QP

This publication is made possible in part by the New York State Council on the Arts with the support of Governor Andrew Cuomo and the New York State Legislature.

TCG books are exclusively distributed to the book trade by Consortium Book Sales and Distribution.

A catalogue record for this book is available from the Library of Congress.

ISBN 978-1-55936-985-5 (paperback)

Cover photo by Jason Hetherington

First TCG Edition, November 2019

Third Printing, August 2023

Contents

Chancing Her Arm

Deborah Frances-White

Thursday 15th November 2012: the remarkable Phoebe Waller-Bridge walked out onto a 'stage' (a platform if we are being generous; a bit of wood if we're not) in the basement of the Leicester Square Theatre in London. There she delivered the first twelve minutes of *Fleabag*.

I had known her for almost a year and had admired the anarchic new-writing events she and her partner Vicky Jones had produced through their company DryWrite. I felt she had the kind of electric energy of someone from the Bloomsbury Set, whom people would tell implausible stories

Phoebe performs the first twelve minutes of what would become *Fleabag* at the London Storytelling Festival, 2012.

about a hundred years after they'd first set London alight, so I was intrigued to see something she herself had written.

With this in mind I asked Phoebe to write and deliver a monologue at our second London Storytelling Festival, produced by my company The Spontaneity Shop. The show was called *Flights of Fancy* and the theme of the stories was 'Chancing Your Arm'. I remember overhearing someone throw this turn of phrase over their shoulder on the Tube and decided it would make some fizzy fodder.

Phoebe said no. She said that it sounded like stand-up comedy and that was a terrifying idea. Admittedly I am a comedian and a lot of stand-up comics were performing at the festival, so I assured her in soothing tones that she could do anything she liked. She hesitated: 'Are you sure it's not stand-up?'

I chanced my arm: 'There's a stool. You can sit down.'

'Alright,' she said, 'I'm in.'

I do not remember why Phoebe headlined the gig, as she felt she had taken a step out of her comfort zone into the direction of stand-up comedy by talking directly to the audience, so in retrospect it seems like we gave her the toughest slot, given that we'd just ruthlessly torn down her fourth wall. I do remember her going on last.

It was a terrific show. Everyone smashed it. Then Phoebe came out and perched on the edge of her promised high stool (which I had brought especially), eyes alight as if she were about to make a hilarious prank phone call. She leaned in to the audience of seventy, as if we were her closest conspirators and confided Fleabag's raciest secrets: her love of slutty little pizzas, her poorly timed sexual urges, her joy in her own hypocrisies and flaws. Just like Phoebe, Fleabag wasn't ashamed of the parts of herself that other women had been trained to find embarrassing – she revelled in them. She found them funny. And we found them funnier. The audience were captivated, thrilled and in hysterics all at once.

After the gig, everyone insisted that Phoebe needed to turn this glorious twelve minutes into a show. We wanted to spend more time with Fleabag, as if we might somehow catch her spirit and adopt her soul as our own.

The first time I saw the full-length show (the text of which you are holding) directed by Vicky Jones for the Edinburgh Fringe, Phoebe came out with Fleabag's gleeful improperness spilling over from the stage into the musty stalls of the Underbelly. But this time there was a new depth in her eyes and dimension in her fingertips.

I felt something open up inside of me while watching her. We didn't have to loathe our kinks. And we didn't have to be in the 'zero fucks' club either. There was a more truthful, meaningful place to find if we could live with the discomfort. Fleabag was wildly crashing about, but it seemed she had accidentally led us somewhere saner than we'd ever been. Phoebe Waller-Bridge, her wiser creator, knew exactly where she was taking us all along.

Fleabag hatched in 2012, and debuted in 2013, just as the fourth ripple of feminism became a wave. Laura Bates created Everyday Sexism. Chimamanda's TED Talk, 'We Should All Be Feminists', went viral. Lucy-Anne Holmes started No More Page 3. Bridget Christie won the Edinburgh Comedy Award for *A Bic for Her*. It was a time throbbing with possibility for women who wanted more and better. It was then that Fleabag emerged sticky with afterbirth, the wriggling, squealing icon of a feminist counter-culture. One hallmark of fourth-wave feminism is women harnessing the power of the internet as a tool of resistance. Fleabag uses it to feed her pornography addiction and order fast food. Her public admission that she'd trade five years of her life in exchange for the 'perfect body' is the ultimate 'I'm a feminist but…'

Fleabag is as sex-obsessed as any Don Draper, as self-obsessed as any Tony Soprano, and as thrilled with her own transgressions as any Walter White. Fleabag's primal scream to feminists is that she is the human deep inside each woman, when the burdensome luggage of gendered expectations is stripped away. She is our hunger to be desired, our desire to be adored and our mistakes that cannot be erased by a million pencil-rubbers. She is our lust, our hypocrisy and our painful longing to be better. Fleabag is the underbelly of our feminism, which is just as real as the glossy top coat. Her mischievous joy makes it possible to look at our own bloody handprint on the wall and think: 'It'll wash off.'

Since 2013 much has happened for *Fleabag*. The live show has been adapted for television and, over two triumphant seasons, has become a spectacular international hit. At the time of writing, the second season is nominated for a gobsmacking eleven Emmys. It has brought us some outstanding insights into relationships – the purest form of violent adoration that only swells up between sisters; the envious passive-aggression you can actually taste from a godmother-cum-stepmother; the unspeakable desire of forbidden coition with the sexiest-possible priest. Fleabag and her attempts at living a braver life have delivered us iconic moments which have deepened our shared understanding of what it is to be human and what it is to be woman, in a world that is constantly rebooting its feminism.

I have no doubt that Phoebe would have written *Fleabag*, that it was erupting from inside of her like a volcano, whether I had pressed her to chance her arm that evening or not, but I feel very privileged to have witnessed its first subterranean outing. I will be part of a generation of women who will forever be grateful to Phoebe because she has allowed us to shed a little of our shame each time we revisit her iconoclastic invention. This book is a lovely way to keep some of Fleabag's lightning in a bottle and, when we need it, in our back pocket.

It seems clear that *Fleabag* will continue to enchant and embolden generations not even born yet, on the page, stage and screen. I hope this story of its genesis inspires any admirer of Phoebe's who is hesitant to step into the light and reveal her emotional connective tissue, to pull up her stool and chance her arm, just in case it turns out she's one of the voices of her generation – and to join the choir of rebels, regardless.

I look forward to telling implausible stories about Phoebe for years to come, that will be retold, ideally with embellishments, a hundred years after she first set London's West End alight.

July 2019

Deborah Frances-White is a stand-up comedian and writer best known for her hit podcast The Guilty Feminist *which has had over seventy million downloads and been performed at the Sydney Opera House, the London Palladium and the Royal Albert Hall. Her book* The Guilty Feminist *is a Sunday Times Bestseller. Her first feature film as screenwriter is the award-winning* Say My Name *released in the US and the UK in 2019. Her play* Never Have I Ever *will be produced in London in 2020. Deborah is currently reviving the legendary Secret Policeman comedy brand in a series of shows and events, as both Creative Director and host, for Amnesty International.*

Introduction to the First Edition

Phoebe Waller-Bridge

I am obsessed with audiences. How to win them, why some things alienate them, how to draw them in and surprise them, what divides them. It's a theatrical sport for me – and I'm hooked.

When Vicky Jones (director of the stage play/inimitable genius/excellent friend) and I were producing nights of short plays under our theatre company, DryWrite, we were forever scrabbling for new ways to put the audience in the centre of the experience.

Each experiment illuminated little tricks of how to construct a satisfying story. We would give briefs to writers, challenging them to elicit a specific response from the audience. It would change each time, but one, for example, was: 'Make an audience fall in love with a character in under five minutes.' Writers would write the monologues, actors would perform them, and each audience member would express their 'love' by releasing a small, heart-shaped, helium balloon at the moment they fell in love with the character on stage.

Each writer could measure their success by how many balloons floated to the ceiling of the theatre during their piece. At the end of the night we'd all then charge to the bar and discuss why some pieces succeeded over others. Whatever the experiment, the audience rarely behaved in the way we expected them to, prompting many fascinating conversations and debates about character, story and language that proved invaluable lessons in playwriting.

Over the years, we put on event after event, experiment after experiment, and at the heart of them were always the big questions about how to affect the audience. How do you make people heckle? How do you make people invest in one character over another? How do you make an audience forgive a terrible crime? There was one I was most intrigued by – 'Funny/Not Funny: How do you make an audience laugh in one moment, then feel something completely and profoundly different in the next?'

It was this tightrope that I wanted to walk with *Fleabag*. When we were developing it for the Edinburgh Fringe, I was obsessively looking for ways to surprise the audience, to sneak up on them just when they least expect it.

I knew I wanted to write about a young, sex-obsessed, angry, dry-witted woman, but the main focus of the process was her direct relationship with her audience and how she tries to manipulate and amuse and shock them, moment to moment, until she eventually bares her soul.

Adapting *Fleabag* for TV meant this same fundamental structure still applied, but experiments with the audience took another interesting turn and Fleabag's relationship with the audience intensified.

In theatre, people come to you, or your characters. In TV, characters arrive in people's living rooms, their kitchen tables, and are often even taken into bed with them! It's a very intimate way of communicating with an audience and a privilege to experiment with. With this in mind, I was determined for the audience of the TV series to feel like they were having a personal relationship with Fleabag – hence the audience address – and the absolute ideal situation was that at the beginning you should feel she wants you there and by the end, that she wishes she hadn't let you in. A feeling I imagine lots of people have felt after spilling it all out to a stranger.

If there is one thing I've learned, it's that you get a lot for free from an audience if you make them laugh. The power of comedy is astonishing to me – how it can disarm an audience and leave them wide open and vulnerable. Ultimately, for the *Fleabag* audience, I wanted the drama of this woman's story to leap into their open, laughing mouths and find its way deep into their hearts.

2016

This piece was originally written for the BBC Daily Drop.

The History of Fleabag

An earlier version of the play that became *Fleabag* was performed by Phoebe Waller-Bridge at the Leicester Square Theatre, London, as part of the London Storytelling Festival, on 25 November 2012.

The first full version of *Fleabag* was produced by DryWrite, and previewed at Soho Theatre Studio, London, on 14 and 16 July 2013, and then performed at the Big Belly, Underbelly, Edinburgh, on 1–25 August 2013, as part of the Edinburgh Festival Fringe, with the following cast and creative team:

FLEABAG   Phoebe Waller-Bridge

VOICE-OVERS
RECEPTIONIST   Francesca Moody
MALE VOICE   Adam Brace
LECTURE-HALL   Charlotte McBrearty
  TANNOY
LECTURER   Teresa Waller-Bridge
BOO (VOICEMAIL)   Vicky Jones
EX-BOYFRIEND   Charlie Walker-Wise
  (MESSAGE)

Writer	Phoebe Waller-Bridge
Director & Dramaturg	Vicky Jones
Producer	Francesca Moody
Designer	Holly Pigott
Associate Designer	Antonia Campbell-Evans
Lighting Designer	Elliot Griggs
Composer &	Isobel Waller-Bridge
Sound Designer	
Associate Sound Designer	Max Pappenheim
Stage Manager	Charlotte McBrearty
PR	Chloé Nelkin Consulting

The production returned to Soho Theatre Studio, London, on 3–22 September 2013.

The production was revived by DryWrite (Producer: Francesca Moody) and Soho Theatre (Producer: David Luff) at the following venues:

Soho Theatre Main House on 7–25 May 2014

Daehangno Small Theater Festival, Seoul, Korea, on 20–23 November 2014

Birmingham Repertory Theatre on 14–17 January 2015*

Tobacco Factory, Bristol, on 20 January–7 February 2015*

The Bike Shed, Exeter, on 10–11 February 2015*

Salisbury Playhouse on 12–14 February 2015*

Tron, Glasgow, on 17–18 February 2015*

The Garage, Norwich on 20 February 2015*

Soho Theatre Studio on 21–22 February 2015*

Sheffield Crucible Studio on 24–25 February 2015*

Traverse, Edinburgh, on 26–28 February 2015*

Live Theatre, Newcastle, on 3–4 March 2015*

Marlowe Studio, Canterbury, on 5–7 March 2015*

Soho Theatre Main House on 5–16 December 2016

Udderbelly, Underbelly, Edinburgh, as part of the Edinburgh Festival Fringe, and British Council Showcase on 21–27 August 2017*

Soho Theatre Studio on 15–18 January 2018*

Sydney Festival, Australia, on 22–27 January 2018*

Brisbane Powerhouse, Australia, on 8–10 February 2018*

Perth Fringe, Australia, on 13–24 February 2018*

Adelaide Fringe, Australia, on 27 February–18 March 2018*

Malthouse Theatre as part of Melbourne Comedy Festival, Australia, on 28 March–22 April 2018*

Wales Millennium Centre, Cardiff, on 26 April–5 May 2018*

Warwick Arts Centre on 8–12 May 2018*

Live Theatre, Newcastle, on 22–26 May 2018*

Sheffield Crucible Studio on 30 May–2 June 2018*

The Old Market, Brighton, on 5–9 June 2018*

* Performances marked with an asterisk were performed by Maddie Rice.

The production received its North American premiere at SoHo Playhouse, New York, on 28 February–14 April 2019. It was produced by Annapurna Theatre, Megan Ellison, Sue Naegle, Skye Optican, Executive Producer: Kevin Emrick, David Luff & Patrick Myles, Barbara Broccoli, Patrick Catullo, Diana Dimenna, Daryl Roth, Eric Schnall, Jayne Baron Sherman, DryWrite (Producer: Francesca Moody) and Soho Theatre; Associate Producer: Bee Carrozzini.

The production received its West End premiere at Wyndham's Theatre, London, on 20 August–14 September 2019, produced by DryWrite, Soho Theatre and Annapurna Theatre, and with the following additional personnel also working on the West End run:

Production Manager	Lloyd Thomas
Assistant Stage Manager	Ben Delfont
General Management	Fiery Angel Ltd
Marketing and	AKA
Artwork Design	
Press	The Corner Shop PR

Fleabag was adapted for television by Phoebe Waller-Bridge, and produced by Two Brothers Pictures for BBC Three, directed by Harry Bradbeer (episode one by Tim Kirkby), and starring Phoebe Waller-Bridge. The first series premiered on 21 July 2016; the second series premiered on 4 March 2019.

It was remade in French for Canal+ as *Mouche*, written and directed by Jeanne Herry, starring Camille Cottin, and premiered on 3 June 2019.

FLEABAG

To Vicky Jones

Note on Text

Other characters can be recorded voices, played by other actors or played by Fleabag.

Pauses and beats are indicated by the space given between lines.

A forward slash (/) indicates where the line is interrupted.

5 a.m. on a roof in East London, photo shoot
for the original *Fleabag* poster, 2013
(Photos by Richard Lakos)

Fleabag rehearsals, 2013

Vicky Jones (director and dramaturg)   Phoebe acting a bit out…

Phoebe, Vicky looking concerned, Holly Pigott (designer)

…and then wondering if that bit should be in it

(Photo by Joan Marcus)

Lights come up on FLEABAG.

She is out of breath and sweating.

FEMALE VOICE. He's ready to see you now.

FLEABAG. Thank you.

FLEABAG *attempts to hide that she is overheating.*

MALE VOICE. Thanks for coming in today. Really appreciate you sending in your CV.

FLEABAG. No problem.

MALE VOICE. It was funny!

FLEABAG. Oh? Okay. That wasn't my intention, but –

MALE VOICE. Great. Our current situation is unusual in that... we don't have many... any women working here. Mainly due to the –

FLEABAG. Sexual-harassment / case.

MALE VOICE. Sexual-harassment case, yes. Are you alright?

FLEABAG. Yes, sorry – I ran from the station. Just a bit hot. Sorry. I'm really excited about –

MALE VOICE. Water?

FLEABAG. No, no. I'm – I'll be okay – I'm – actually, yes please, that would be great.

Over the next speech, FLEABAG *pulls her jumper
halfway over her head exposing her bra. She realises she
doesn't have a top on underneath and she attempts to
pull her jumper back down as if nothing had happened.*

MALE VOICE. So we are looking for someone who can
handle themselves in a competitive environment. It will
mainly be filing, but we have some pretty good filers so
– Haha – yeah. It also involves updating the website
and throwing up an occasional twit. It says here that
you have done something similar before at the… café
that you used to –

Ah okay. Um.

I'm sorry. That won't get you very far here any more.

FLEABAG. Oh no – sorry – I thought I had a top on
underneath.

MALE VOICE. Yup. Okay. But for the record.

FLEABAG. No seriously. In this case – genuine accident.

MALE VOICE. Look. With our history here I understand
why you might have thought –

FLEABAG. I wasn't trying to – Jesus – I was hot –

MALE VOICE. I take this kind of thing very seriously now.

FLEABAG. I'm not trying to shag you! Look at yourself.

MALE VOICE. Okay. Please leave.

FLEABAG. What!? But I – you don't understand. I need –

MALE VOICE. Please just leave.

   FLEABAG *starts to leave. She turns back.*

FLEABAG. Perv.

MALE VOICE. Slut.

FLEABAG. Wow.

MALE VOICE. Please leave.

FLEABAG. You please leave.

MALE VOICE. It's my office.

FLEABAG. Yeah?

MALE VOICE. Okay.

   Sound effect of feet walking away and a door opening.

FLEABAG. Wait.

   Footsteps stop.

   –

   FLEABAG *turns to the audience.*

Three nights ago I ordered myself a very slutty pizza.

I mean, the bitch was dripping.

That dirty little stuffed-crust wanted to be in me so bad, I just ate the little tart like she meant nothing to me, and she loved it.

That pretty much nailed that, and it was pretty late now, so I dragged myself upstairs and got into my office –

or… my bed – and tried to work on the figures for the café. I run a guinea-pig-themed café. But it's out of cash and it's going to close unless a cheque falls out of the sky, or a banker comes on my arse, but neither are going to happen, and I don't want to dignify the banker-man with a proper mention so I'm not going to talk about him or how I do sometimes wish I could own up to not having morals and let him come on my arse for ten thousand pounds, but apparently we're 'not supposed to do that', so okay. I *won't*. Even though it would solve *everything*. I won't.

Even though I could.

Lying in my office, the café numbers start to jump out at me like little ninjas, so I rationalise it would be good to just switch off for a bit. Improve my mind. So I watched a pretty good movie, actually, called *17 Again* with Zac Efron who is… fit.

I know.

But seriously, he's actually a – a really good actor. So – Yeah, and the film could have been worse – honestly. Check it out.

Then that finished. So I lay there. Thinking. Café. Numbers. Numbers. Zac. Numbers.

Googled Obama to keep up with – y'know. Who, as it turns out, is also – attractive.

Lay there. Numbers, numbers, Obama, numbers, Zac, Obama, numbers, Zac –

Suddenly I was on YouPorn having a *horrible* wank.

Found just the right sort of gangbang.

Now that really knocked me out, so I put my computer away, leaned over, kissed my boyfriend Harry goodnight and went to sleep.

—

I wake in the morning to find a note from Harry, which reads

'That was the last straw.'

Which is… pretty out of the blue if I'm honest. Didn't know he was counting straws. But nice to know he was paying attention. All his stuff was gone. And everything in the fridge. I was a bit thrilled by his selfishness. Suddenly fancied him again. But relieved one of us did something – he used to say things to me like

HARRY. You're not like other girls… you can… keep up.

FLEABAG (*ponderous*). Keep up.

I stood staring at a handprint on my wall from when I had a threesome on my period. Harry and I break up every twelve to eighteen months and when we do, well…

I wish I could tell you my threesome story was awkward and sticky and everyone went home a little bit sad and empty, but… it was lovely.

Sorry.

I admire how much Harry commits to our break-ups. The fridge is a new detail, but he does always go the extra mile. A few times he's even cleaned the whole flat.

Like it's a crime scene. I've often considered timing
a break-up for when the flat needs a bit of a going-over,
but I never know what's going to set him off. Keeps me
on my toes.

I sit on the loo and think about all the people I can have
sex with now.

I'm not obsessed with sex.

I just can't stop thinking about it.

The performance of it. The awkwardness of it. The
drama of it. The moment you realise someone wants
your body... not so much the feeling of it.

I've probably got about a week before Harry comes
back. I should get on it.

Okay.

Into the shower. Boom. Bedroom. Make-up. Boom.
Gonna really make an effort. I take half an hour trying
to look nice and I end up looking... *amazing*. I mean,
best in ages. One of those days. Boom.

Gorgeous, fresh-faced, heels, wearing a *skirt*, new top,
little bit sexy, on my way to *save my* café and yes, I am
strutting.

I see a man walking towards me from the bus stop. He
can't take his eyes off me. I'm all walking like I've got
a paintbrush up my arse, thinking:

Yeah, check me out, cos it's never gonna happen,
Chub Chub.

—

I opened the café with my friend Boo. She's dead now. She accidentally killed herself. It wasn't her intention, but it wasn't a total accident. She didn't think she'd actually die, she just found out that her boyfriend slept with someone else and wanted to punish him by ending up in hospital and not letting him visit her for a bit. She decided to walk into a busy cycle lane, wanting to get tangled in a bike. Break a finger, maybe. But it turns out bikes can go fast and flip you into the road. Three people died. She was such a dick. I didn't tell her parents the truth. I told her boyfriend. He cried. A lot.

—

Chub Chub's getting closer. Oversized jacket. Meaty face. Looks me up and down. It's like he's confused about how attractive I am – he can't quite believe it. I worry for a second I'm going to make a sex offender out of the poor guy. He's about to say something. Here we fucking go, this better be good. He's passing, he's passing. He clears his throat, brings his hand to his mouth and coughs:

CHUB CHUB. Walk of shame.

FLEABAG. It's too late to go home and change. I have some flat shoes in my bag and anyway, he's fat.

And he can't take that off at night.

—

Harry's a bit fat. He lightly pats his belly, like he's
a little bear. Proud of what he's achieved. Hunted.
Gathered. Eaten. Pat. Evidence. Pat, pat. It makes me
laugh. A pretty girl at a party once asked me if I secretly
liked that Harry had a little paunch, because it made
him less attractive to other women. Her boyfriend was
the whale in the corner, blocking the door to the toilets.

I asked her if he made her wash the bits he can't reach.
She slapped me. Actual slap.

Which means he did.

–

Boo's death hit the papers.

'Local café girl is hit by a bike and a car and another
bike.'

There was a buzz around the café all of a sudden.
Flowers, notes, guinea-pig memorabilia were left
outside in her memory.

Boo made sense of the guinea-pig theme. She was all
small and cute and put pictures of guinea pigs
everywhere. I pretend they're not there. Which I suspect
makes the whole guinea-pig-café experience a bit creepy.

Boo was built a bit like a guinea pig. No waist or hips.
Straight down. She rocked it. And she was *beautiful*.
Tricky though. Jealous. Sensitive. But beautiful and…
my best friend.

–

Ten past eleven at the café. Quiet. Eerily so. Boo always
used to play music, read out horoscopes and shrivel crisp

packets in the microwave. Used to make the place stink, but she'd turn the little packets into key rings and give them to the people who were especially polite.

One guy in the corner drinking tap water and using the plug. He should buy something, but it's just nice to have someone around. He's reading. He's quite attractive actually, but he doesn't look at me. Even when I purposefully drop a cucumber so I have something to bend over for.

Even Joe hasn't turned up.

Joe's always here at eleven. Proper old geezer, cockney from the toes up, one of life's good people. Huge teeth, white hair, ludicrous grin and a joy that slaps you in the face until you can't help but smile at it. Even the fucking furniture loves Joe. I swear the door swings open voluntarily when he arrives, if only to give the man an entrance. Suddenly he'll just be there. *CRASH*. It almost clatters off its hinges with the force of him.

Nothing touches Joe. He's invincible. You can hear him bellowing 'ALLO, SWEETPEA' to the whole street before he swaggers in, long white hair blowing behind him, cut-off checkered trousers and white T-shirt with braces, dripping wet from the rain all:

JOE. Alright, magic. What a beautiful morning! I can't get over how glorious it is out there. Lucky to live, eh. Lucky to live.

FLEABAG. I don't know what he does. I just know he comes in at eleven.

Usually.

Find myself watching the door. Didn't notice he was such a regular when Boo was here, but now…

But then it's okay, because I see his silhouette take up the window and wait for the door to crash open. But today it just flops to its side with a whimper and Joe limply shuffles to the counter.

I'm not prepared for this.

Alright, Joe?

JOE. Yeah... yeah. I'm alright, ducky.

FLEABAG. Tea, Joe?

JOE. Yeah lovely, lovely. Thank you, darlin'. I'm just gonna... be out the back.

FLEABAG. I make his tea. Six sugars. I take it outside and place it on his little table. He rolls a fag and watches the cup steam.

JOE. Now, ain't that a beautiful thing.

FLEABAG. Not sure what to... I ask him for a rollie. I don't smoke. Well I do, but – shut up.

Can I have a rollie, Joe?

JOE. Sugarplum, you can have anything you want. May I have the honour?

FLEABAG. Yeah, thanks.

He rolls it with his spindly, inky fingers. Takes four seconds. Proper pro. I take it and light it. We smoke.

I sit beside him. Two of us on tiny little kids' chairs –
sort of a gimmick thing, but really they were cheaper.
He looks ridiculous.

JOE. I *love* these chairs y'know.

FLEABAG. What's... wrong, Joe?

JOE (*sighs*). Ah my girl, I just... I love people. I *love*
people. But... they get me down.

FLEABAG. Yeah. People are... shit.

He turns and I can see into every deep line on his face.

JOE. Oh no, darlin'. People are *amazing*, but... when will
people realise... that people are all we got?

FLEABAG. He smiles, but I feel a bit ambushed. I pretend
I have to wash the cappuccino machine, go inside and
wipe the nozzle a bit.

–

Five o'clock. Northern line. I'm trying to read an article
about how the word 'feminist' has apparently become
dirty. I try to engage, but it just makes me think of a
bunch of dirty little feminists. I snort-laugh at myself,
and then catch the eye of an Attractive Looking Man.
Oooh. Well, he is attractive when holding his paper up to
here – it all gets a little rodenty from the nose down, but
good enough for some eye-fucking on the Tube. He
smiles at me with his tiny mouth. I smile back.

He looks down. I look down.

Then we both look up at the same time!

Little giggle. Other people in the carriage start to notice, *charmed* by the moment.

It's revolting.

The Tube is pulling in to Tottenham Court Road.

We both stand up at the same time.

I could vomit.

He says

TUBE RODENT. This doesn't happen very often, does it?

FLEABAG. I give a horribly giggly 'No! No, I suppose it's… quite… rare… yeah…'

He says this may sound crazy, but he has this crazy idea and the crazy idea is to take my number.

We give credit to the moment and exchange numbers.

–

I come out of the Tube and have a Harry panic. He just – won't be there any more. Madam Ovary is telling me to RUN BACK TO SAFE PLACE. YOU CAN MAKE BABY IN SAFE PLACE. But I've got to ride it out. He'll text me later. The fridge means nothing. Ride it out. I met a nice rodent on the Tube. I have a lot to be thankful for.

–

FEMALE VOICE. Welcome to Women Speak. The lecture will commence in five minutes. Please have your tickets ready.

FLEABAG. I find my sister outside the lecture hall. She is uptight and beautiful and probably anorexic, but clothes look awesome on her so...

Mum died two years ago. She had a double mastectomy and never really recovered. It was particularly hard because she had amazing boobs. She used to say I was lucky because mine will never get in the way. When I asked her what she meant she used to demonstrate by pretend-struggling to open the fridge door, or pretending not to be able to see what's on the floor.

My sister's got whoppers. But she got all of Mum's good bits.

Dad's way of coping with two motherless daughters was to buy us tickets to feminist lectures, start fucking our godmother and eventually stop calling.

These lectures are every three months. It's virtually the only time I see my sister. She looks tired. We sit in the waiting room. I realise I'm wearing the top that she 'lost' years ago, so this is going to be tense.

She really fucking loved this top.

Her eyes fix on it. But – and I can see her brain ticking – she decides to bank it for later. Makes me nervous. Ammo.

She's reading her 'Kindle'.

She's done her hair a bit fancy, I wonder if she's going out after the lecture or if she's just got her period. She always does something a bit different around her period. She gets really bad PMT. Mum called it a Monthly Confidence Crisis, but it's PMT. The only way she can get through it is to reinvent herself in some small way.

One particularly bad month, she came into the kitchen on the brink of tears, in full Lycra. Even Dad had to leave the room. She looked like she'd climbed into a condom. It was an emotionally complex couple of days, which we're not allowed to talk about any more.

She's sitting so still. She's definitely having a monthly confidence crisis. I mean it's in plaits. Both sides. Sort of tied at the top. It's unbearable. I can't resist.

(*To* SISTER.) Hair looks nice.

SISTER. Fuck off.

FLEABAG (*to audience*). Brilliant.

She asks about work and I get all spiky. I tell her the café's lease is up in two days unless I can find at least five grand, which is impossible. So I'm having to deal with letting go of the only thing I have left of Boo, and the only thing that's going to save me from becoming a corporate lady-slave like her, and that I know everyone thought I'd fuck it up, and now it looks like I've fulfilled everyone's expectations, which I didn't mean to say, it just falls out, and now I'm gonna get her smugness all up in my face.

She just looks at me. No reaction.

I know the rules, so I ask her about *her* super-high-powered, perfect job-work-super-life. She tells me she's finally been offered the wet-dream of a job in Finland. Apparently they want to overpay and underwork her and she won't have to wear power suits any more.

(*To* SISTER.) Wow. Finland!

But she's turning it down, because her husband says she shouldn't go, because of Jake.

Jake is her stepson. He's really weird, probably clinically, but no one really talks about that. He freaks out if she's gone for longer than a day and he's got this thing about trying to get into the bath with her. He's fifteen.

I tell her

(*To* SISTER.) He's not your son.

SISTER. That's not the point.

FLEABAG *makes a face*.

Don't make that face.

FLEABAG. I didn't make a face. Go! This is about *you*.

SISTER. I knew you'd say that.

FLEABAG. I tell her she's making a mistake, she shouldn't let other people get in the way of what she really wants and Finland is what she really wants.

She tells me her *husband* isn't 'other people'. That her *husband* is her life.

I tell her her *husband* tried to touch me up at Christmas.

I don't know why I said it. It's true, but he was drunk so…

Martin's always drunk. Which is odd because she is so straight. Maybe that's not odd. But he's very good at being drunk, in that he's FUN DRUNK! No one wants to admit there's a problem, because then they don't get to have 'crazy nights out' with 'fun drunk Martin' any more.

(*Scottish accent*.) Martin.

He's one of those men who is explosively sexually inappropriate with everyone. But then makes you feel bad if you take offence because he was just being FUN. You can tell him you are 'popping to the loo' and he'll say –

MARTIN. Aye you pop to the loo, then pull your little knickers down and I'll come in and FUCK you!

FLEABAG. Claire always tries to sort of half-laugh like she gets the joke, which isn't even a joke.

FEMALE VOICE. Welcome to Women Speak. Sorry for the delay. The lecture will begin shortly. There is no food or drink permitted in the auditorium.

FLEABAG. She just stares at me.

Then her neck goes red. I've only see that happen once before.

Then she stares ahead of her.

I give her half my sandwich. Which she eats! Maybe she isn't anorexic... maybe clothes just...

Bitch.

We just sit and wait. Eating the sandwich.

Can't read her. Never been able to read her.

She pulls out a card from Dad and puts it on the seat between us. It's probably still there.

FEMALE VOICE. Women's Speak is about to commence. Please enter the auditorium.

Sound of hubbub.

FLEABAG. The lecture hall is huge. We go right to the front and sit down. Still can't read her.

Suddenly she says

SISTER. I'm going to go to fucking Finland.

FLEABAG. Okay.

SISTER. I hate these suits.

FLEABAG. Okay.

SISTER. How much do you need to save Boo's café?

FLEABAG. About five grand.

SISTER. Okay. I'll transfer it tomorrow. But I don't want to come to these any more.

FLEABAG. Okay.

SISTER. And I want my top back.

FLEABAG. Okay. Thanks, Claire.

Sound of a female lecturer testing the mic. FLEABAG *pays attention.*

LECTURER. Gosh look at you all! Thank you so much
for coming. I am overwhelmed by how many faces
I see before me. I hope I do your efforts justice with
what I have to say this evening. But before I begin,
I want to ask you a question. The same question that
inspired me to give this lecture. The same question that
was posed to women all around this country with, well
frankly, shocking results. Now, I don't know about you,
but I need some reassurance. (*Little laugh.*) So, I pose
the same question to the women in this room today:
please raise your hands if you would trade *five years* of
your *life* for the so-called 'perfect body'?

FLEABAG *throws her hand in the air.*

FLEABAG. Both of us.

Four hundred women stare at us, horrified.

We are *bad* feminists.

After the lecture Claire says she's going home to talk to
Martin.

I want to ask her if she'd have a drink with me before
she goes, but I don't know how, so I just watch her
plaits disappear into the crowd outside the Tube.

—

Text from Rodent

TUBE RODENT. Still smiling! Smiley face.

FLEABAG. Aw.

I text back: You free now?

He is. We meet up and get very, very drunk. I can't stop staring at his tiny mouth – he is telling me a story like he doesn't want to let the words out.

He tells me his sister is deaf, which is his way of letting me know he is interesting and sensitive. Which is fine. But then he is the only one in his family who didn't learn sign language so... Apparently, because they grew up together, she can lip-read him. Which makes me wonder what she thinks he is saying all the time, because to me it looks like Oooo OOOoo Oooo.

He says his sister is so instinctive. She can read people brilliantly. How she'd be able to read me.

He's having an *excellent* time.

–

Harry has terrible instincts. Once – I think this may be the best thing he has ever done – Once, he went to a restaurant – he's quite shy really – he went to a restaurant having had a filthy night out with me the night before. I mean, the man was *hanging*. He was having lunch with these important website bods, when it hit him. Halfway through the starter. Yeah. He was gonna be sick. Like, now. He excused himself, and hurry-walked to the loo. He burst in – knowing by now that this was going to be a projectile affair – but all the urinals were taken and all the cubicles were locked and he couldn't bring himself to spew in a sink so, in a panic, he kicked down the door of one of the cubicles revealing a man having a shit. Then boom. It just aaallll caaaame ooouuut – he puked all over the guy sat there, all over his shirt, his cock, his legs, his hands, his boxers, the wall, round his ankles, drenched him.

But then – and this is the best bit – in the frenzy of it all,
Harry rationalised –

HARRY. Oh God, I've just puked on this guy – he is
going to punch me.

FLEABAG. So he smacked him in the face.

Isn't it beautiful? It was particularly good because
when he first told me and Boo he didn't know it was a
funny story. It will never be heard like that again. It
was such a serious story. He was *mortified*. Boo loved
poo stories, so couldn't actually deal with the glory of
this one. She just stared, open-mouthed, paralysed with
joy as he told it.

–

A few weeks ago, when Harry thought I was sleeping
he rolled over, stroked my hair and whispered

HARRY (*whispered*). Where have you gone? Where have
you gone?

FLEABAG. He thinks I'm neglecting him, but when your
heart is – I wish he'd just fuck me. All he wants to do is
make love.

He's wasting me. I was once fucking a man who would
breathe on every thrust, 'you're so *young,* you're so
young.'

I masturbate about that all the time. I masturbate a lot
these days. Especially when I'm bored or angry or
upset or happy.

–

Sound of the Tube.

Last Tube. Attempting to kiss Tube Rodent. It's like target practice with a very small moving target.

I ask him back to mine, but he says he's got work tomorrow.

I say I can come back to his, but he says it's an early start.

I say I'll get him a cab to work in the morning, but he says that's ridiculous.

I say 'what the fuck's your problem' and he says nothing he'd just like to see me again, not rush.

I tell him he's a prick. He says he's 'not sure what's going on'.

I tell him he's a pathetic excuse for a man and leave him at the barriers. Ha.

It's a bit weird then, because we have to come down the same escalator. Push my bum out a bit. Give him some perspective.

I turn around at the platform, but he's gone.

—

At the end of the platform, sat on the bench thing, is the drunkest girl I have *ever* seen. Head rolled forward, tit hanging out, bag sprawled. Nicely dressed, normal-looking girl who had clearly just had one hell of a night. Last Tube rolls in. She doesn't move. I nudge her awake and she stumbles onto the carriage only to slump into a seat, head rolling, other tit folding out now, bag tangled in her feet. I ask her where she is getting off, she says

Slumps back, mouth open. No movement.

DRUNK GIRL. 'Waterloo.'

FLEABAG. Okay, my stop. I help her off, I ask her where she needs to get to next.

DRUNK GIRL. London Bridge…

FLEABAG (*to* DRUNK GIRL). Okay.

DRUNK GIRL. And then Kent.

FLEABAG. Tubes are finished, so we are finding an Overground to London Bridge. At one point, we are walking, and she just falls flat on her face. Boom. Get her up. Keep going. Her head is going all over the place. I'm trying to keep her talking. After about forty-five minutes – *forty-five* – we are on an escalator, there is a bit of a lull. Then she turns to me and says

DRUNK GIRL. Aw… you're such a lovely man.

–

FLEABAG. Her train pulls in. I don't let go of her.

I ask her if she'd rather come home with me, but she just says

DRUNK GIRL (*grinning*). How dare you… Naughty boy… no!

FLEABAG. So I push her on the carriage and she's gone.

–

I leave the station and think, 'what's one more'. I go into a bar. It is a *business* bar. People are doing *business*. I drink a lot and pretend I am in *business*. A sweaty, bald man cups my vagina from behind at the bar. But he buys me a drink so – he's nice actually. After a while he disappears and the business bar closes. (*Slurring slightly.*) Closed for business. Shutting up shop.

That's what Boo said every time we closed the café.

BOO. Shutting up shop!

FLEABAG. Like she was drunk. Which we often were. We'd close up, sink a bottle of wine. Boo would play the ukulele and we'd make up filthy songs. For hours.

(*Singing.*)
'Another lunch break, another abortion.
Another piece of cake, another two, fuck-it, twenty cigarettes.
And we're happy, so happy to be modern women.'

–

Suddenly I'm at a familiar doorstep. I ring the bell. And ring the bell. And hammer at the door. And yell like a goat. This should be humiliating. Howling through a man's letter box in the middle of the night, but I'm rolling with it.

A light goes on. I see his silhouette as he trudges down the stairs. He must recognise mine through the door, because his body language changes suddenly. He slowly unhooks the latch and opens the door.

He looks like shit.

I put my hand right over his face and push it a bit.

Strikes me as something I'd never thought I'd do to a parent, but it feels right at the time.

He stands in the doorway. Boxer shorts. T-shirt. I can see the shape of his little manboobs.

(*To* DAD, *very drunk*.) Alright, Dad!

DAD. What's going on?

FLEABAG. Oh, I'm absolutely fine.

DAD. Okay.

FLEABAG. I just –

DAD. Yes?

FLEABAG. Nothing.

DAD. Okay?

FLEABAG (*drunkenly*). Okay… I don't… yeah… I… uh… um… It's a… hm… ah, fuck it.

I have a horrible feeling I'm a greedy, perverted, selfish, apathetic, cynical, depraved, mannish-looking, morally bankrupt woman who can't even call herself a feminist.

He looks at me.

DAD. Well… You get all that from your mother.

FLEABAG (*to* DAD). Good one.

I wonder if he'd find me attractive. If I wasn't his daughter.

(*To* DAD.) If you saw me on the internet. Would you click on me?

DAD. I'm going to call you a cab, darling.

FLEABAG. He lets me wait in his living room while he calls me a cab. I can hear my godmother trying to be quiet at the top of the stairs.

When the cab comes he gently puts me into it and gives me twenty quid.

–

I'm in a *cab*. I can go *anywhere*. So I tell him to take me to… my *flat*.

Already thinking about what I'm going to look up.

–

Back at the flat. I turn on the TV and cry for a bit.

–

I think about a girl called Lily, who I used to touch a bit when we got drunk. Harry didn't know, but girls don't count. I text her. She lives quite close, I think.

Suddenly I'm on PornHub, wet as a beach towel, but I can't get there because the girl has spots on her arse. Some of them just don't make the effort.

—

Nothing back from Lily. I start thinking about this ginger guy I met at a festival last summer.

It was a month after Boo died. I'd taken a pill, and flown off into the woods. I was desperate to get away from Harry. He had started to hug me relentlessly, telling me how much he loved me, asking how much I loved him, checking if I was 'okay'. There was a rave in the wood. I was panicking and touching my face a lot. And suddenly he was there – ginger guy. He told me to follow him. That he'd take me back to my tent. We were walking for ages. He was holding me by my wrist. At one point he picked me up. It was very dark. I couldn't work out where we were. He wouldn't put me down. He was holding my legs really tightly. Said I was too weak to walk and that I had to trust him. Eventually we stopped. I felt him lie me down in a tent on my back. And then he... he...

He put a cover over me, and a bottle of water by my arm and sat outside until I fell asleep.

Thought he could have at least tried to touch me up a *bit*. Never quite let that go.

—

I text him. Tell him I'm single and horny. He gets back saying he's out, and can be here in twenty minutes. Great. Quickly drink half a bottle of wine, shower, shave everything. Decide I'm going to up my game a bit. Dig out some Agent Provocateur business – suspender belt, the whole bit. Open the door to him. 'Hellooo.' We get to it immediately. After some pretty standard bouncing, I realise he is edging towards my arsehole. I'm drunk, and owe him a 'thank you' for being nice to me at the festival, so… I let him. He's thrilled.

The next morning I wake to find him sitting on the bed, fully dressed, gazing at me. He says that last night was incredible – which I think is an overstatement – but he goes on to say it was particularly special because he has never managed to actually… up-the-bum with anyone before – to be fair, he does have a large penis – and although it was always a fantasy of his, he'd never found anyone he could do it with. He touches my hair and thanks me with genuine earnest. It's sort of moving. He kisses me gently. I kiss him back. Then he leaves.

And I spend the rest of the day wondering…

Do I have a massive arsehole?

–

Five to eleven at the café. I'm still thinking about it.

Haven't heard from my sister. No transfer yet. Wonder if Martin's murdered her, and is now stalking round the city looking for me.

The door smashes open. Joe.

JOE. ALLO, SWEETPEA!

FLEABAG. His legs are too long for his body.

JOE. Look at this beauty!

FLEABAG. He holds up a ukulele that someone just gave him in the pub last night.

Just gave him a ukulele.

He says he's written a song.

I don't want to hear it.

He pulls out another ukulele that apparently another person gave him in another pub.

JOE. Crazy 'ow the world speaks to you all at once eh!

FLEABAG. He says he'll sing his song to me. Then he'll teach it to me. So we can both sing it to Hilary.

I tell him I'm too busy and sit out the back until I hear him leave.

He tinkles a bit, but I don't hear him sing.

–

Schoolkids used to come to the café. Mainly because of Hilary.

Basically, I'm shit at presents and for Boo's birthday two years ago I panicked and bought her a guinea pig. She called it Hilary and now I'm stuck with it.

I don't feel anything about guinea pigs. They're pointless. But Boo took Hilary very seriously as a gift. And then everything became guinea-pig related.

–

I think she was just relieved to have a different animal associated with her. When she was about five, she mentioned, on a childish whim, that she liked owls. For the rest of her life she got owls. Owl duvet covers, owl pens, books about owls, trips to owl sanctuaries. She fucking hated owls. Show her an owl and she'd lose her shit. What she really liked – and I knew this – was screwdrivers. Crazy about them. We'd spend hours unscrewing things, then screwing them back up. She slept with screwdrivers under her pillow until she was about ten.

Come to think of it, a screwdriver would have been a better present than a guinea pig.

–

Midday. Still haven't heard from my sister. Martin's going to hate me. I picture his massive, Scottish head. Hope he hasn't beaten the shit out of her or anything. No, he'd never do something as sexy as that.

I'm joking. Jesus.

–

Hilary is fat and ginger with frizzy bits. Like Annie, the orphan. If she was grown up. And fat. And a guinea pig. Which – well, who knows what became of her.

She has this punky bit of fur that explodes off the crown of her head and falls down over her eyes. Makes her look pretty badass. She has a very straight expression. Boo always said, if Hilary was in a band, she'd be the guitarist who takes the music really seriously. She did take music seriously actually. Whenever Boo played stuff in the café she'd be all –

Plays some beats. Nods almost imperceptibly, in time with the music. No expression.

She's also a sneaky little shit. She knows how to open her hutch door. I've seen her do it. She pushes the little wood stopper until it drops out and the door just swings open. She then freezes, as if she hasn't done anything, then she actually *turns around* – and lowers herself down onto the counter, little legs kicking, looking over her shoulder – checking… checking… She often does a little poo in the excitement. Once landed, she creeps along the counter all the way to the window. Then, when she gets there, in her frenzy of freedom, she sits down and looks out. Watching the world.

If she wants me to think she's really profound and poetic doing that, I'm not rising to it.

–

Apparently guinea pigs need other guinea pigs. Or they can die of loneliness.

But Hilary didn't need a mate. She got more than enough attention. The punters loved her, she was always on someone's lap, and she had Boo, who never left her alone. They adored each other. The morning Boo's boyfriend told her he'd fucked someone else… she walked right past me, took Hilary out of her hutch and sat out the back with her for hours.

I once read a story from the paper to Boo and Hilary about how a little kid repeatedly stuck rubber-ended pencils up the class hamster's arsehole, because he liked it when their eyes popped out. He was sent to a juvenile bootcamp.

I read it out as a bit of a joke really, but Boo was *distraught.*

BOO. They sent him away? But he needs help!

FLEABAG. She was a surprising person.

(*To* BOO.) Yeah. He pencil-fucked a hamster.

BOO. He's obviously not happy. Happy people don't do things like that.

FLEABAG. Fair point.

BOO. And anyway, that's the very reason they put rubbers on the ends of pencils.

FLEABAG (*to* BOO). To fuck hamsters?

BOO. No, because people make mistakes.

FLEABAG. But now Boo's gone it's a death café so no one comes in any more. Hilary just sits in her hutch like a lump. Staring at me. I don't know what to do with her.

–

Six o'clock. Two yoga-body girls come into the café and order risotto off the menu. I pop to Tesco. Microwave their economy meal. The girls were talking about never wanting to give birth, because of what it'll do to their sex lives.

Still haven't heard from my sister.

I put an empty crisp packet in the microwave and watch it shrivel.

Play with my phone for a bit.

–

BOO (*recorded voicemail*). Hi this is Boo. I can't come to the phone at the moment but leave a messiagio and I'll get back to you.

FLEABAG. Someone should probably disconnect that.

–

I start texting Tube Rodent. I apologise and apologise and eventually send him a picture of my tits. He sends me one back. I *think* it's of his cock.

–

My boyfriend before Harry used to make me send him pictures of my vagina wherever I was. Ten or eleven times a day. I'd have to go and lunge in a disabled toilet and take an attractive picture of my vagina. Which is not easy, on the whole. Specially as he always wanted the worm's-eye view. It often looked like someone had dropped a little bap, on its side, on the floor of a hairdresser's. Then taken a photo of it.

One temping morning, he asked me to take photos of my 'favourite bits of my body'.

I go to the disabled loo.

Mimes unbuttoning her top. No expression. Bored. Takes pictures of her breasts. Stands up. Mimes hitching up her skirt, pulling aside her knickers, takes pictures of her vagina. No expression. Bored.

Mimes buttoning up. Flicks through the photos. No expression. Bored. Chooses one. Send.

Puts phone away.

Beep beep.

Takes phone out.

EX-BOYFRIEND. Oh that is so hot. Send another one, you beautiful bitch.

Mimes unbuttoning her top. No expression. Bored. Takes pictures of her breasts. Stands up. Mimes hitching up her skirt, pulling aside her knickers, takes pictures of her vagina. No expression. Bored.

Mimes buttoning up. Flicks through the photos. Bored. Chooses one. Send.

Puts phone away.

Beep beep.

Takes phone out.

Now say something so dirty you shock yourself. Send me another picture. Oh God, I'm wanking.

FLEABAG. It exhausted me, but you've got to do it. Can't have them looking elsewhere.

The boss banged on the disabled-loo door. It was my fourth visit that morning.

BOSS. Is everything alright in there?

FLEABAG. He's Australian.

(*To* BOSS.) Yeah – I've – I've just – got cystitis.

BOSS. Oh you poor chickadee! My wife gets that all the time! Cranberry juice is what you need. Buckets of it. Shall I get you some from the canteen?

Hon?

Hello?

Are you crying?

–

FLEABAG. I'm going to stop waxing. I met a man who said – I say 'said' it was more of a yell really – how much he loved a 'full bush' and how 'rare they are these days'. Although it was inappropriate at the time – family friend at Mum's funeral – it filled me up with something. Hope? Relief? I don't know. Can't bring myself to grow one.

–

I call Tube Rodent. He comes to the café with a bottle of wine. We drink it.

He whispers to me

TUBE RODENT. I have an enormous penis.

FLEABAG. I say: really? He says

TUBE RODENT. Yeah.

FLEABAG. I say: well that's lucky, because I have an enormous vagina. He says

TUBE RODENT (*confused*). Awesome.

FLEABAG. We fuck behind the counter. He's very bony. All corners. It's like having sex with a protractor. He doesn't come. He says I'm being too intense, whatever that means.

We turned the lights off and it's quite dark now. He's pulling on his trousers, looking for his phone to see if his friends are going out later. He's wearing this pink-and-purpley paisley scarf. He looks like a lady.

He hops over to the window and leans on the sill. He turns his phone on and he screams. Really high-pitched. The light from the phone made Hilary's eyes flash red in the darkness. She must have wandered over to the window while we were having sex.

For a second I laugh at his reaction, but she moves, and he screams again. She tries to run towards me, but she panics and sort of slips off the side. She lands on her stomach and struggles a bit, but Tube Rodent sees red and kicks her.

She flies against the wall with a thud.

He stares at the furry pile on the floor.

But she twitches. It makes him jump. He kicks her again.
She goes flying across the floor.

I can't move. I think about Boo. I think about them
playing together.

Tube Rodent's panicking. Mumbling something about
a rat phobia.

I tell him he can go, and he disappears.

Hilary is on her front, but her back is to me. She looks
like a… furry bullet.

She's still alive, but…

I put her back in her hutch and we just sit for a bit.

–

I text arsehole guy. He texts back saying he has a
girlfriend and was really drunk the other night, but
would love to hang out in a non-sex way. Sorry if he
led me on.

I send my ex a picture of my vagina.

I send Harry a picture of my vagina.

I text Lily.

Still nothing from my sister.

Hilary's not moving.

BOO (*recorded voicemail*). Hi this is Boo. I can't come to
the phone at the moment but leave a messiagio and I'll
get back to you.

FLEABAG. Hilary starts making a horrible, chattering
noise. I take her out of her hutch again. I put her on my
lap. I stroke her, but she doesn't stop. I put her back.

–

I go to The Rabbit and Winslow pub. I smoke outside.
Three people are laughing by the door. I can just make
out the braces and the white hair through the crowd.

I can hear him.

Someone's let him on stage with his ukulele. He's
singing a song. People are laughing and clapping.

I listen to it from outside. It's about a train ride he once
took through Ireland, where a man told stories to
everyone about love and home and romance and
adventure and surprises and beautiful women and
beautiful men and mothers and daughters and fathers and
sons and monsters and fairies and parties and wishes…

All the usual crap.

The whole scene is something out of a revolting
romcom, but he's nailing it.

He goes to the bar afterwards. Everyone buys him drinks. The man doesn't need to work.

I realise I've forgotten to give Hilary her Earl Grey.

–

Ten thirty at night. I hammer and hammer and ring the bell. I can see his silhouette at the top of the stairs but he doesn't open the door.

–

Back at the flat. Harry has obviously been round. The TV has gone and it smells like he did a shit. He never used to shit in the flat. He was really weird about it. Used to go to the pub over the road.

–

I sit on my stripy sofa. Open my laptop.

Anal

Gang bang

Mature

Big cocks

Small tits

Hentai

Asian

Teen

Milf

Big butt

Gay

Lesbian

Facial

Fetish

Young and old

Swallow

Rough

Voyeur

Public

Suddenly the sun's creeping in and I'm raw.

Lease is up today. Still nothing from my sister. I leave the flat.

–

BOO (*recorded voicemail*). Hi this is Boo...

–

FLEABAG. I put the closing sign up outside the café.

Three minutes past eleven. He's not here yet. I watch the door.

Ten past.

The door flies open.

JOE. Alright, baba ghanoush! Forgive me – I'm a little late, but do I have a morning story for you today or what! Listen to this –

FLEABAG. I tell him to shut up and close the door. He looks confused. But he does it.

(*To* JOE.) Why do you come here, Joe?

JOE. What?

FLEABAG. I close the blind. Lock the door.

(*To* JOE.) Why do you come here, Joe?

JOE. Tea, love. See my ladies!

FLEABAG. Hilary's still not moving.

(*To* JOE.) It's okay, Joe. I understand. There's nothing wrong with you.

I take off my top. Unhook my bra. Place them gently on the counter.

He stares at me. I step forward. Showing him my young tits.

He shuffles a bit. His breathing changes. He's trembling.

He moves his hand up.

–

Nine o'clock that morning. My sister's door.

Martin's looking down at me.

MARTIN. Hello, you.

FLEABAG. Is Claire here?

MARTIN. Aye.

FLEABAG. I try to get past him into the house. He doesn't let me.

Claire comes to the door. She's crimped her fringe. I deliver a beautifully constructed joke about it. She snaps at me. Says I have to stop talking to people like I'm doing a stand-up routine. That some things just aren't fucking funny.

I laugh. And then I don't laugh. My throat goes dry. No one says anything for a bit.

(*To* SISTER.) You didn't transfer the money…

SISTER. No.

FLEABAG. You're not going to Finland.

SISTER. No.

FLEABAG. Why is he still here?

SISTER. He didn't touch you.

FLEABAG. He tried.

SISTER. He said it was more like the other way round.

FLEABAG. That's not true.

SISTER. How can I believe you?

FLEABAG. What? Because I'm your –

SISTER. After what you did to Boo.

FLEABAG (*to audience*). That wasn't my fault. He wanted me… he… wanted me so…

—

It's eleven fifteen now.

Joe is shaking.

I'm standing. Topless. Just the right angle.

His hand keeps rising, until it rests on his eyes.

JOE. Put your clothes back on, darling.

FLEABAG. What?

JOE. Put your clothes back on.

FLEABAG. Come on, Joe. I'm not going to judge you.

JOE. I come here for my tea, darling. And to see you. That was a sad thing that happened to your friend.

FLEABAG. You're weak.

JOE. That may be true, but... I'm going to go now.

FLEABAG. Stay. Come on. Please. Joe. I'm twenty-six years old, Joe.

He stops. He brings his hand down from his eyes. He finally looks at me.

JOE. Go home, darling. I'm sorry. This ain't my bag.

FLEABAG. I grab his arm as he walks past. He's thin but baggy. His skin pinches in my grasp. It's disgusting.

The door closes behind him.

–

I sit on Joe's chair for a bit. There's something not right about that man.

Hilary's teeth are going again. Crashing against each other. The noise is unbearable. Relentless chattering. They do that when they're distressed or angry or I can't listen to it. I take her out of her hutch. I hold her little body to my naked chest. I can feel her claws. She can hardly move. Her bones feel bent and her breathing is shallow. But her teeth are going like – she won't – I stroke her body. I look into her face through her ginger, punky bit. I imagine sticking my finger in to make her eyes pop out. I imagine it. I imagine doing that – I can't imagine doing anything else and as my hand moves down her body – I – I –

When I first gave her to Boo she was so tiny. I put her in a little gift box from a crappy card shop. She just sat there on a bit of cotton wool. Looking up through her tiny punky bit. She was ridiculous. A little overexcited fuzzball. She'd just sit in your hand like – (*Makes a mini-explosion sound.*)

Boo's face. Boo's face when she opened the box – a huge grin spread across her whole body.

BOO. What is this!? Is this a guine– Did you get me a – What – What is this!?

FLEABAG. I don't know. Something to love?

I'm crying. My fingers are gripping her. I can't – I imagine my – I can't – I can feel how scared she is. How much pain she's in – My fingers are – I can't – I hold her to me tightly and – I hold her to me tighter... I hold her to me tighter, until I feel her bones crack against me and her chattering stop.

Everything is quiet and she is safe.

–

MALE VOICE. Okay. Please leave.

FLEABAG. What!? But I – you don't understand. I need –

MALE VOICE. Please just leave.

FLEABAG *starts to leave. She turns back.*

FLEABAG. Perv.

MALE VOICE. Slut.

FLEABAG. Wow.

MALE VOICE. Please leave.

FLEABAG. You please leave.

MALE VOICE. It's my office.

FLEABAG. Yeah?

MALE VOICE. Okay.

Sound effect of feet walking away and a door opening.

FLEABAG. Wait.

Footsteps stop.

What made you laugh?

MALE VOICE. What?

FLEABAG. On my CV. You said it was funny.

MALE VOICE. Um. You wrote that you run a café for guinea pigs…?

FLEABAG. Right. That's not strictly true but, okay. That made you laugh?

MALE VOICE. Yes. I suppose. Never thought guinea pigs needed –

FLEABAG. It was a guinea-pig-themed / café.

MALE VOICE. Oh right.

FLEABAG. Yeah.

MALE VOICE. That makes sense.

FLEABAG. Yeah.

What if I wrote that I fucked that café into liquidation, that I fucked up my family, I fucked my friend by fucking her boyfriend, that I don't feel alive unless I'm being fucked and I don't feel in control unless I'm fucking, because fucking makes the world tighten around me, that I've been watching people fuck for as long as I've been able to search for it, and that I know that my body as it is now is really the only thing I have and when that gets old and unfuckable I might as well just kill it, that sometimes I wish I never knew fucking existed because somehow there isn't anything worse than someone who doesn't want to fuck me.

That I fuck everything. But *this* time, I genuinely wasn't trying to – I wasn't – I was –

Either everyone feels like this a little bit and they're just not talking about it, or I'm completely fucking alone. Which isn't fucking funny.

MALE VOICE. That really wasn't appropriate.

FLEABAG. Yeah. Okay. Sorry.

She goes to leave.

MALE VOICE. Look. Three months ago I touched a colleague's breast at a party. Not for the first time. It's ruined the reputation of the business I've been building my whole life and has completely alienated me from my family.

FLEABAG. Why did you do it?

MALE VOICE. I... It was a terrible... mistake.

FLEABAG. People make mistakes.

MALE VOICE. Yes they do.

FLEABAG. That's why they put rubbers on the ends of pencils.

MALE VOICE (*little laugh*). Is that a joke?

FLEABAG. I don't know.

MALE VOICE. Shall we… start this interview again?

FLEABAG. Okay.

MALE VOICE. Thanks for coming in. Really appreciate you sending in your CV.

FLEABAG. No problem.

MALE VOICE. It was funny.

She laughs.

FLEABAG. Fuck you.

End.

(Photos by Joan Marcus)

Behind the scenes…

A Conversation Between
Phoebe Waller-Bridge and Vicky Jones

Phoebe: Remember when we spent every single second of every single day temping and coming up with new theatre nights?

Vicky: I do! Almost from the moment we met! Aah, what a journey.

Phoebe: So, where did *Fleabag* start for you, Jonesy?

Vicky: For me it started with that stand-up night you agreed to. You said you'd written this short piece and it was 'sort of stand-up comedy, but sort of drama'. We were rehearsing *Mydidae* by Jack Thorne, and you asked me if we could look at it at lunchtime. I couldn't believe you wanted to do stand-up of any form and I thought you were mad for putting yourself out there, but once you actually read the piece out to me, the voice of this character just filled me up. She was so funny and acerbic, and flawed and amazingly compelling at the same time. You had written in a rhythm which just totally jumped out. This young woman was in so much pain and so much self-denial, but she was so *funny*. That was the first time I heard Fleabag's voice!

Phoebe: I was so excited to show it to you. I wrote it solely to make you laugh. I love the challenge of facing an audience; how much is required to surprise and entertain them. But, really, you were the only audience I cared about… and had. Haha!

Vicky: Aaaw. I think it's amazing how you have this absolute love of your audience, but you're fearless with them. You're constantly thinking about how they will feel from moment to moment, and you never apologise for really going there to keep them on the edge. Actually, you're really rough with your audience, but they love you for it. Hah!

Phoebe: You brought that out of me. The truth is, I was totally lost when I left drama school. When I started, I thought I knew what exciting acting was, what exciting theatre was… but by the time I left I had lost that spontaneity. I'd worried so much about nailing the technical elements that I'd forgotten how to be playful. I went into the industry thinking it was all about getting acting 'right', but I didn't know how to do that except to have Shakespearean hair and know where my diaphragm was. I think I was too young to understand the training then, or wanted to please everyone too much, but the experience left me a bit creatively frozen. But then I met YOU!

Vicky: Ahhhh! Oh dear, this is bringing out a total love-in between us.

Phoebe: Yeah baby! When we met I felt like that old fire was lit in my belly again. We spoke for so long about what we thought was fun and dangerous and often boring about theatre – and how our main job is to surprise an audience. I remembered that my focus as an actor was to convince an audience, not impress them. I'd forgotten that.

Vicky: We *did* talk endlessly about all those things though, and truth was at the heart of it. Getting truthful reactions from audiences was everything. We developed these ideas that gave the audience a role as individuals – to be active in their experience of watching theatre. To have to judge what they were seeing in some way. The only thing we required from them was to be honest. That was exciting. I remember seeing your eyes light up when we got the idea exactly right. We were literally trying ideas out on each other, and it was only when we both got excited that we knew it was right. We weren't trying to please anyone else.

Phoebe: It taught us so much about writing. Do you remember Surprise Ninja?

Vicky: I do!

Phoebe: The rule was – if a scene could be improved by a surprise ninja bursting in and fighting everyone, then the scene isn't interesting enough. Haha.

Vicky: Tough rule, but an effective one. So much of what we learned on those nights went into *Fleabag*. Even bits of your early short plays.

Phoebe: Yes! The lecture scene. We were so tickled by the idea of two women raising their hands at the question 'Would you give up five years of your life for the perfect body?' that we just kept acting it out for each other over and over again. You still do it better than me. Those moments of the process are the most joyful. When you don't really care what anyone else thinks. It cracked *us* up and felt important to *us,* so that's all that counted.

Do you remember much of the first *Fleabag* rehearsals?

Vicky: Some things. You hadn't written it when we started.

Phoebe: I just have blurred memories of pitching stuff to you, feeling sick with panic, you rightly storming out one day because I was being so negative about the scraps I *had* written, us having to share lunch nonetheless, and that girl at Starbucks giving us two iced coffees even though we could only afford one. That girl. I'll always love that girl.

Vicky: That girl! She knew! She knew we were doing something special and for a good reason! You had booked another job during rehearsals, and you were panicking. I convinced you to cancel that job, even though you felt awful about letting those people down. But you were so relieved you had, because writing *Fleabag* in two-and-a-half weeks was about the hardest thing you had ever done. Not just because it's almost impossible to write a play in that time, but because you *knew* her. You knew what you wanted her to be, but it was like you were dragging her from the depths of your belly and you were SO hard on yourself. So much incredible material got chucked out, and you nearly threw the whole thing out altogether out of sheer frustration, because you couldn't quite do justice to what was in your heart. *That* was why I stormed out! But you came and found me, and we had a little cry. That was when we tried to get coffee and that Starbucks girl gave us a free one because we looked so emotional, and then we went back and you finished writing it. Actually, let's be honest… you finished it on the train on the way up to Edinburgh. That final line that was eluding you…

Phoebe: Oh god yeah. I knew I didn't have the cut-to-the-heart-of-the-play line and it was killing me! Then you just said, 'What do you *want* the line to be?' I replied with the line from the end about being completely alone. You looked at me for a beat then said, 'JUST WRITE THAT THEN!!!' Haha. Then we couldn't find a pen. Jesus. Carnage.

Vicky: You've always found it last-minute though.

Phoebe: True. You're a much more disciplined writer. I envy that.

Vicky: It's not discipline you lack. You just won't compromise your vision and you won't rest until you think it can't be improved! I remember sitting on the floor with Char [*Charlotte McBrearty, stage manager*] through rehearsals and having constant pins and needles because we didn't have any chairs. And Char's laugh: a 'Chartle'. It was always good when you got one of those.

Phoebe: Haha, the CHARTLE! I lived for that sound. If a line got a Chartle, the line got in the script. I've got to say though… you did much more than direct this play. We've joked that we have been each other's muses, but you're even more than that. Being in that room, me coming in every day and reading stuff out… you would always see to the core of what I was *trying* to write, even when I couldn't. You would push me to discover it by asking the most left-field questions about the character, forcing me to articulate her. Sometimes I would bring in an idea or a line and it wouldn't make sense. But you would tweak my performance, lace it with sadness or hardness… and suddenly the character would emerge again. It was the most important collaboration of my life. Do you know what I mean… it felt more than simply directing it, right?

Vicky: Ahh, yes it was thrilling, I've never been more excited. I was dreaming her, I was thinking about her all the time, and all your instincts, combined with our total freedom – not having to please anyone – we could test all your instincts and we could just be totally honest about what got to us or didn't. Your tendency to want to surprise people – that featured massively, so the character would lead you one way and then gut-punch you with a line which was just the last thing you were expecting. You would test it on me and I remember the thrill of being totally in the palm of your hand, even when I knew what you were going to say. I think we've always had a passion for the tiniest details, so we would happily talk for hours about the nuances of this girl and how she spoke, so it was an experience of developing the text and performance at the same time – like a real person being created. And the ideas were just pouring out of you, so every morning we had so many to mould and build or discard. But I remember your trust in me, in Char, in Cesca [*Francesca Moody, producer*] and Iso [*Isobel Waller-Bridge, composer and sound designer*]. If we liked it, you did it. If we didn't react in the way you hoped, you threw it out. You had zero ego about any of it.

Phoebe: Remember the night you locked me in the room 'until it's finished!!'? Haha.

Vicky: Yes! I hardly ever tell you what to do. But I had to tell you to JUST FINISH IT!!! Remember us recording all the voices in the cupboard?

Phoebe: Yes, with Iso! Oh god, making Tube Rodent sex sounds and you recording Boo's voicemail. I love that you play Boo. It helps me pretend to cry at the end.

Vicky: Hahahaha! You're not pretending!

Phoebe: Performing the final speech does get me riled up but, I'm afraid to say, imagining a life without you is what gets me to that broken place at the end of the play. Imagining your death. That's nice, isn't it? What was the scariest bit of directing *Fleabag* for you?

Vicky: Arriving in Edinburgh. It was terrifying because we hadn't really rehearsed it. You'd just been writing it so we had vaguely set what you were gonna do, but we didn't know it at all. You were learning it, learning it, learning it on the way up and I didn't know what the venue was going to be like, we had never been to Edinburgh before, we were told we had three hours of tech and it was in the middle of the night, so all of that was pretty scary. I think the worst moment was when they decided not to tell us that the *Guardian* and the *Telegraph* were in on the first night and I found out just before and you did the show and you missed out a chunk and I went backstage after the show and you were like 'Yeah, I blanked and that's a shame, but hey we did it, we got through it right?' and then you were told that the most influential critics had come to see it and therefore would probably never ever see it again and you just sat with your head in your hands. That was the worst moment for me of the whole entire thing by miles. It was horrible. And then it was okay. Like… really, really okay. Haha.

Phoebe: Coming on the first night is harsh, guys. Give us a break!

Vicky: Oh! Also Horn Star!

Phoebe: Oh my god, they made me fucking sit on a cow and have my photo taken. We'd all been – hold on, I don't know who I'm talking to now, I'm supposed to be interviewing you.

Vicky: Well, tell me about it, I'll pretend I didn't know.

Phoebe: You just like hearing the story…

Vicky: Yes I do.

Phoebe: Haha okay. It was my first interview about *Fleabag* and I was so excited. We'd finished the chat and then I was asked to 'come take some photographs'. Now, we had known from playwriting folklore that if someone asks you to take your photo, there are certain mortifying inevitabilities to be aware of. They will either ask you to sit backwards on a chair, lie down with a leg up or lean moodily against a brick wall with a hand on your face. I had been warned. So far on this shoot we were brick-free and I'd been vertical most of the day. We got some decent photos of me sitting on a bench with my legs up and stretched out, but it could have been worse. I thought I'd gotten away with it. As we were on our way back though, the photographer slowed down. He had spotted a massive, plastic, purple cow in the middle of the Underbelly square. I looked at him. I saw the idea forming, then: 'Hey Phoebe, why don't you get on the cow?' I remember thinking, 'This is it, this is the moment. This is it.' Firstly, this means I must officially be a playwright. Secondly, I can't say no because I am too British and grateful that anyone wants to take a picture of me at all. I just remember looking at him pleadingly. There were loads of people eating lunch around the cow. Then he said, 'Look. Yesterday someone ran around in a chicken suit for me and no one said anything.' I didn't know what to say, I just knew it felt wrong…

Vicky: Haha. And then didn't the PR person come up to you…

Phoebe: Oh yes! She walked up saying, 'Heeeey Phoebs, it's totally fine!' and I whispered, 'I don't know if I wanna do this' and she just looked at me, dead in the eye, and said, 'Just shut up and get on the cow.'

Vicky: HAAHAA!

Phoebe: Thank you. That expression has since been used extensively by our team as shorthand for 'Oh fucking get on with it'! Of course I scrambled onto it and of course they used the picture of me on the cow. All the photos on the nice bench vanished. But *then*… in the interview I talked about how casually women get sexualised in the media and the massive headline over me sitting on the back of this massive purple cow was 'Horn Star'!!! Way to kick a girl when she's on a cow.

Vicky: It was a betrayal, wasn't it? It had felt like you had such a great interview.

Phoebe: Lessons, lessons! It's all silly really, but at the time it burns! Do you remember that we rehearsed *every day*? We went out a lot – because you have to in Edinburgh – but my god we still got up in the morning and worked the play all day too.

Vicky: It was brilliant though because we would have the feedback of a whole audience to base our decisions on, so actually we were honing it with dozens of previews, which is when you really learn about a play. So although we were effectively experimenting on the first Edinburgh audience to come and see it, we made the play way more solid through all of that I think. I remember Steve Coogan was in the audience near the end and we were like 'Oh my god, Steve Coogan is in the audience' and he was really laughing! Some really thrilling things happened during that time. I'll never forget when we got five stars in the *Scotsman*. We had to celebrate, so we went out for an incredible breakfast. None of us could believe it.

Phoebe: Yes! We shared a cooked breakfast, I remember everything about that breakfast.

Vicky: And I remember the morning you got the Fringe First and we got all dressed up and stood kind of awkward on the platform so chuffed.

Phoebe: Haha, those photos!

Vicky: And then when you got the *Stage* Best Performer over all of those other ones that had done so unbelievably well and all the big shows that had done brilliantly in Edinburgh had been nominated and we had been nominated and you won. We all said afterwards that when they announced that you won, the world slowed down like 'Phoeeeebbbbbeeee Walllleeerrrr-Brrrriiidddggge'. It was just like so amazing, it was the penultimate day of the show and it was the best way to end the festival, you won the Best Solo Performer.

Phoebe: God, the whole thing was so thrilling, wasn't it? Taking *Fleabag* to Edinburgh with our tiny team felt like true freedom. I always come back to that. It was the first time we did something completely on our own... and *that* happened. Then coming back to Soho Theatre and there was one original preview that we had done there, the one we must not talk about the ending of, there was an alternative ending for the play very early on which is not for now.

Vicky: It shall not be mentioned.

Phoebe: It shall not be mentioned, there are eighty people in the world that think Hilary came to a very different kind of end.

Vicky: I've just always felt, even then... that as long as nothing came to spoil it, *Fleabag* was going to work. The special feeling started early on, but the nerves didn't go away for ages. I was sort of, just knowing that it had to be exactly right, that there was exactly a way to do this and that was something between you and me. I've never felt more ambitious about anything, I don't think.

Phoebe: I know. For however shambolic we'd seem to be, we were perfectionists about it. We all were. Iso would ask for a sound effect to be half a beat quieter or you would want an extra beat before a line. It became about creating something *perfect*, even though we knew that was impossible, it's always worth getting as close to it as possible. Even the tiniest looks, you used to give me notes about like 'Remember when you did this, try slowing this down a touch, try looking into the distance for a second longer and don't let the audience off the hook quite yet and then…' oh god, the 'Guinea Pig Gasp'!

Vicky: Oh god, yes, the Guinea Pig Gasp. When that gasp happened we were like 'What was that?! How did we get that gasp?' And we went back and tried loads and loads of different ways and about three or four nights later, you got it and tried it out and got the gasp!

Phoebe: That first one was hilarious. They gasped, then I gasped because they gasped! I remember feeling 'This should have more impact.' You were forensic in trying to get it back. You'd give me tiny notes: 'Try this rhythm, this pause' – then BOOM. We got it!

Before we opened, we were getting a lot of advice from people about how to stage a one-person play. We were told the only way to keep it interesting was for the actor to be up and moving around a lot. We tried me bounding around for the first few rehearsals until you went all badass and 'Fuck this shit, no, I'm really sorry, I just always imagine you, sat on a stool and doing nothing. You don't need to move, you just need to focus.' It felt so rebellious that you had said that because it went against the advice that every *single* person had given to us!

Vicky: I was really aware that we were going against people that I respected and saying, 'We might be mad, but we have to trust ourselves here.' It's just what felt right. I knew that you were engaging enough, and I knew we wouldn't want a distraction from the story. I felt the same when we were looking at it on the Wyndham's stage [*for the West End run*]; I don't want anything but a light on you. I just want to watch you being this character and I am so happy that we didn't try and change it with some sort of physical malarkey.

Phoebe: Me too. I only stand up three times in this one and it's exhausting. When we were about to open in New York, you had just given birth to your gorgeous boy, and couldn't come out for the run. Even though we had done the show so many times and Char, you know, Char is a boss and makes sure the timing is so tight, and Cesca keeps the whole thing running and keeps our spirits up, but I felt the absence of you in a sort of profound way. Back in the day you watched every performance. I would worry that if you weren't in there… if we removed that magical piece from its perfect place it would all fall apart! So in New York, feeling a little disconnected after so many years having not done the play, I sent a message saying I couldn't quite find her yet and was feeling a little lost. You wrote me this unbelievable text message. It made me cry when I read it because it cut right to the core of *Fleabag* again. I'm not the only person who knows this character inside out. All of us on this team do, but I think possibly most of all you, because you've looked at her from the inside when you were dramaturging it, you looked at her from the outside when you were directing me and you looked at her and defended her from every other point of view.

Your text was a roar about what that character meant to us back then. Bringing her right back into the present for me. I read that text every single night before I went on stage because it distilled everything that we'd tried to create with this show. You said, 'I don't think she's felt anything in a really long time' – Jesus, it makes me emotional just saying it – 'and she hasn't allowed herself to feel anything in a really long time. *That's* who you need to perform.' Before I met wonderful Harry [*Bradbeer, director of the TV adaptation*], a lot of directors we met for the TV show had a very different take on her – i.e. she's cold, she's fucked-up, she lets it all hang out, her vagina's on her sleeve and her heart's up her arse and all that kind of stuff. But you and I just saw her as we see each other… as someone we could easily become if we went down a slightly different road or had had our hearts broken in the way she did. She is desperately trying to convince the audience that she is fine and in control, but the truth is she lost her best friend and no longer has anyone who understands her in the world.

Vicky: Well, you know this character means the absolute world to me. She came from your heart and you had such pity for her and such compassion, but she was so fucking funny and she didn't ever feel sorry for herself –

Phoebe: And that's the key!

Vicky: She didn't have any compassion or pity for herself, she was just *funny.*

Phoebe: Yay, Fleabag! I'm going to miss her.

Vicky: Me too. Go Fleabag at the Wyndham's!

Phoebe: She'll go out with a bang. So to speak.

Vicky: Haha. She will.

August 2019

'Shut up and get on the cow.'
© Bev Johnson (IG: Beverlylove)

The Creative Team Looks Back

Here is the *Fleabag* family. They weathered script-free production meetings, non-existent budgets, wet festivals, sleeping bags in living rooms, shared beds, countless builds, sound studios in cupboards, national tours in backs of vans – and this show would never have got here without them. Every time we remount the show we consider changing something... the size of the stage, the colour of the top, the timing of a cue, the brightness of the lights... and every time we rediscover that everyone's first instinct was the right one. The production has been exactly the same – bar a couple of line changes – since the very first one.

This is a little window into their journeys with *Fleabag*.

P.W-B.

Francesca Moody
Producer

Trust your instincts, and don't panic. These are the two most enduring lessons I learnt producing *Fleabag* for the first time in 2013.

Whenever I'm reading a new play now, I'll always seek out that same feeling I had the first time I read *Chancing Your Arm*, Phoebe's short piece of comedy storytelling, which eventually evolved into this show. I didn't know what *Fleabag* was about, but I did know it was going to be good.

Producing a play which is unfinished is not an easy task – at times I'd go as far as to say it was fully terrifying, especially when, the week before rehearsals started, Phoebe admitted she hadn't actually written the play yet... In fact, rehearsals were essentially Phoebe writing the play and Vicky dramaturging it. As the producer you have to keep a calm head and I did my level best never to let anyone see how nerve-wracking it was for me – although there is a now-infamous story about the time I visited everyone in rehearsals, cool as a cucumber, left happily and then minutes later Char, our stage manager, found me breaking down in the broom cupboard.

I'd worked at the Edinburgh Festival in some capacity every year since I was seventeen so was confident I had a handle on how to lay the foundations for a successful show, even if we didn't know what it was yet: a bold image ('Let's put Phoebe in a Batman suit on the roof of a building at 5 a.m. and take a picture for the poster'), the right time-slot ('Let's put the show on at 9.30 p.m. so we're a funny theatre alternative to all the stand-up'), interesting copy ('Let's make sure we include the phrases "porny-wank" and "lovely threesome" in the marketing blurb'), the right venue ('Let's go to a space with a small capacity so we can definitely sell all the tickets'). I'm not saying that all those things made *Fleabag* the success it was in Edinburgh, but they definitely gave us a good head start.

Since Edinburgh, *Fleabag* has been to London, around the UK, South Korea, Australia and New York. I've eaten chicken feet in South Korea and sat behind Kevin Bacon whilst he watched the show in New York (the 'Six Degrees'!). The long-term success of the play would be nothing without the partnerships we have formed along the way, first with Soho Theatre and later Annapurna. I am and will always be a huge advocate of co-production for that very reason. Soho Theatre were the original *Fleabag* cheerleaders and our co-production with them following the original run meant (especially early on) we were stronger in contacts, resources, people and money.

Mostly, what I love about *Fleabag* is, that despite the different theatres and places it has been, we have always produced exactly the same show we did back in 2013. So now, producing *Fleabag* is as much about protecting the integrity of what we created then, in that quite frankly magical, messy and life-changing summer.

Charlotte McBrearty
Stage Manager

I'm beyond proud to have worked on *Fleabag* from day one, rehearsing in a disused office block on Whitechapel High Street with no running water. When Francesca asked me to come on board, I knew it would be good, and thought it would be a fun way to spend the summer, but I didn't anticipate the many lives it would touch and how much of an effect it would have on each person involved.

I remember sitting at a table seat on the train from London King's Cross to Edinburgh in July 2013 with Isobel, Vicky and Phoebe, frantically rubbing out every single cue I had already painstakingly written into the script, as half the structure was changing, things were being cut, things were being added, and thinking to myself, 'This is going to be a nightmare.' It wasn't.

Phoebe only called for a prompt once, and the energy in the audience was unreal every night. The most interesting part about stage-managing this show is that you feel like you're acting with the performer. There are about a hundred sound cues in the show, all meticulously timed. Before every performance Phoebe and myself run the beginning and end of the show with each other to get in sync, the same way two actors would. You have to be sensitive to how the audience are reacting, as if I'm even a beat late or early with a cue it can really throw a scene off-balance. I've travelled to some beautiful places and countries doing this show – I learnt how to say 'massive arsehole' in Korean but have since forgotten – and I'll never forget myself and a team of about fifteen people having a thirty-minute international conference call about the transportation of the *Fleabag* Chair from London to New York.

A particularly heart-warming moment during this process was at Soho Theatre, overhearing an older woman say to an usher after the show: 'Please let her know she's not alone.'

Elliot Griggs
Lighting Designer

Rehearsals were a bit of a blur as I was also doing tech work at the Opera House during the day (and overnight) to pay the bills. However, I do remember laying on the grass in the green-room tent at Latitude (where we previewed the show) where Phoebe was scribbling extra bits in the margin of the script. I also remember there being three of us trying to sleep in the lounge of the flat where we were staying in Edinburgh.

I loved lighting the show because without a big set, all the changes of location and times of day had to be created by Iso and myself. But it's all done carefully with just a few subtle colours and angle changes. When I first designed *Fleabag*, we were in a tiny studio with no budget. So I had to be creative with only twenty-four lanterns, including the audience house lights, to create all twenty different times and locations. At the mouldy damp arch 'theatre' in Edinburgh, we only had twelve, which I had to rig and cable myself from 11 p.m. overnight. I tried scaling up the rig as the show got bigger, but we found it didn't need it. The colours were fine-tuned a bit to nail the feelings we wanted, but it's the simplicity of the show that really makes it. For our final West End run, the number of lanterns is still pretty much the same as the very beginning, albeit a little bit fancier.

I've been so happy every time I've heard that the show has been coming back out. It's always felt like a team effort, right from when we were all doing it for no money right through to it becoming a worldwide phenomenon!

Holly Pigott
Designer

I was first approached about *Fleabag* in May 2013 with an extract, maybe three or four pages long, of a piece that DryWrite were developing for the Edinburgh Fringe. I was working as a design assistant at the Royal Shakespeare Company at the time and was instantly seduced by the refreshingly honest and witty character of Phoebe's writing.

The process of making the show was very unique as the script was still being written. It meant that my work as designer had to be very sensitive to the evolution of the text, something that led us all to work in a very organic and collaborative way. I would say that the design is the embodiment of the KISS (Keep It Simple, Stupid) principle, which for the character of Fleabag is perfect in many ways.

After several long conversations over coffee and wine (and slutty pizzas) in Soho where various brilliant, and probably not-so-brilliant ideas were thrown around, we always came back to the importance of the text over anything else. The principle of keeping the space clear and minimal was an acute choice to give Fleabag the platform she needed to deliver the story exactly as it was written to be.

Isobel Waller-Bridge
Composer & Sound Designer

When we started making the sound for *Fleabag* we knew two things: we had £100, and a script demanding a café, a Tube train, three different pubs, a lecture hall, a lonely flat, London streets, a shower, a taxi, Dad's house, a guinea pig, a sex scene and loads of characters despite there being only one performer and a chair. We needed a sound design to take us seamlessly from place to place, and person to person. We wanted each effect to feel naturalistic, and as distinct from each other as possible. For example, the bell for Fleabag's café door had to be specific enough so we instantly knew where we were, but it also helped reveal the mood of the characters entering the café. When Joe is in a good mood, it rings out powerfully as he flies through the door. But when he's sad, it tinkles softly.

We had to create a makeshift recording studio with duvets on the walls to substitute for a real one. Everyone who made this show is in the fabric of the sound design. We couldn't afford to book actors back then, so turned to friends, family and production team. Phoebe, Vicky and I crammed ourselves into a tiny cupboard to record bum slaps for the Tube Rodent sex scene; our mum recorded the lecturer's speech in her kitchen; I played the ukulele under the duvet; 'Welcome to Women's Speak' is our stage manager Char, Francesca voiced the receptionist and Boo is played by Vicky Jones!

When the show transferred to London we were given a budget to re-record professionally. We spent an hour in the studio, only to admit to each other that we all preferred the original duvet recordings, which have been used in every single show since.

One of the main challenges was deciding how the show should be cued. We needed Phoebe to be completely in control of the rhythm of the words as she moved through the worlds of the play, but also needed room to change the rhythm if she wanted to. Char McBrearty's laser-sharp comic and dramatic timing quickly became key to this. After some trial and error, we found that every cue, no matter how small, had to be triggered individually. There are over a hundred cues in the show and what people don't see is how instinctively Char and Phoebe play off each other all the way through the performance.

This collaboration has been the most fun imaginable. I'm so glad we're back together for the West End run. It's a strange feeling to do a run of this play without all of us having to share a bed, but I'm excited!

© Faye Thomas

About the Author

Phoebe Waller-Bridge is a multi-award-winning creative, garnering praise for her work as an actor, writer, creator and showrunner. Following its smash debut at the Edinburgh Festival Fringe in 2013, the London run of Waller-Bridge's one-woman show *Fleabag,* which she wrote and performed, earned her an Olivier Award nomination, a Special Commendation from the Susan Smith Blackburn Prize and the Critics' Circle Award for Most Promising Playwright, among other accolades. In 2019, *Fleabag* opened Off-Broadway at New York's SoHo Playhouse. The extended, sold-out run earned her a Drama League Award nomination for Distinguished Performance, a Lucille Lortel Award nomination for Outstanding Solo Show, and a Drama Desk Award nomination for Outstanding Solo Performance.

Fleabag was also adapted into a critically acclaimed television series, which earned Waller-Bridge a BAFTA Television Award for Best Female Performance in a Comedy Programme. The second season of *Fleabag* aired in the UK on BBC Three and on Amazon Prime in the US, receiving tremendous critical praise. The series received eleven Primetime Emmy Award nominations and six wins including Outstanding Comedy Series. Waller-Bridge won for Outstanding Lead Actress in a Comedy Series and Outstanding Writing for a Comedy Series.

Waller-Bridge also garnered acclaim as the writer and showrunner of the first season of the celebrated BBC America television series *Killing Eve,* starring Sandra Oh and Jodie Comer. The series earned Waller-Bridge a Golden Globe Award nomination for Best Drama Series, as well as an Emmy Award nomination for Outstanding Writing of a Drama Series. The first season won a Peabody Award in the Entertainment category, and was also nominated for fifteen BAFTA Television Awards, for which it won Best Drama. Waller-Bridge serves solely as an Executive Producer on the second season of *Killing Eve*, which received nine Primetime Emmy nominations, including Outstanding Drama Series. BBC America recently renewed the series for a third season, which Waller-Bridge will executive produce.

In March 2019, HBO gave a series order to the eOne romantic comedic thriller *Run,* starring Merritt Wever and Domhnall Gleeson, written by Vicky Jones. Waller-Bridge will executive produce the series alongside Jones under DryWrite.

Additional notable television credits include *Crashing,* which was her screenwriting debut, and *Broadchurch*. On film, Waller-Bridge appeared as the first female droid in Ron Howard's *Solo: A Star Wars Story*.

Waller-Bridge's additional theatre credits include *The One* (Soho Theatre), *Mydidae* (Trafalgar Studios), *Hay Fever* (West End), *Tribes* (Royal Court), *Rope* (Almeida), *2nd May 1997* (Bush Theatre, Evening Standard Theatre Award nomination for Best Newcomer), *Like a Fishbone* (Bush Theatre), *Sixty-Six Books* (Bush Theatre) and *Roaring Trade* (Soho Theatre).

Waller-Bridge is also Co-Artistic Director of DryWrite Theatre Company, an award-winning and Olivier-nominated new-writing theatre company that challenges writers to work with specific briefs and goals to actively engage audiences. She is also a graduate of the Royal Academy of Dramatic Art.